YOUNG REPORTER IN FRANCE

HAVING FUN

On s'amuse

SUE FINNIE AND DANIÈLE BOURDAIS

Franklin Watts

This edition 2014

Franklin Watts
338 Euston Road
London NW1 3BH

Franklin Watts Australia
Level 17/207 Kent Street
Sydney, NSW 2000

Series editor: Sarah Peutrill
Art director: Jonathan Hair
Designer: Graham Rich
Photo manager: Véronique Bussolin
Photographs by Paul Villecourt, unless otherwise specified
Text consultant: Fabrice Blanchefort

Thanks to Carine Bourgogne, Fabrice Blanchefort and Jean-Maxime Fangous for their
contribution to the audio recordings.

The authors would like to thank the following for their help with research on the Young Reporter
in France series: Françoise Cordero, Nathalie and Julie Schmidt, Maria and Juliette Lorcy-Robin
and the children of Crest.

Credits: AFP/Getty Images: 10bl. Arpi/Shutterstock: 27t. Petur Asgeirsson/Shutterstock:
8tr, 28tl. Bayard Presse: 22c. Roi Brooks/Shutterstock: 11c. Eric Fougere/VIP Images/
Corbis: 12t. Fourgeot/Shutterstock: 10tr. Maksym Gorpenyuk/Shutterstock: 11t. holbox/
Shutterstock: 10tl. Tamara Kulikova/Shutterstock: 26b. Little Marcel, littlemarcel.com:
18b. Stuart Monk/Shutterstock: 10cl. Monkey Business Images/Shutterstock: 18t, 29b.
Thomas M Perkins/Shutterstock: 23b. Photocreo Michal Bednarek/Shutterstock: 21tc.
Sylvain Roussillon/Franco Folies: 12b. courtesy of Stephan Rudolph, www.flickr.com/
photos/stephanrudolp h: 13. semaine-bleue.org: 27c. stockfolio®/Alamy: 11b. Pierre
Verdy/AFP/Getty Images: 12c. Viapresse: 22cb. Thierry Zoccolan/AFP/Getty Images:
27b. Every attempt has been made to clear copyright. Should there be any inadvertent
omission please apply to the publisher for rectification.

Dewey number: 306.4'81'0944
ISBN: 978 1 4451 3217 4

Printed in China

Franklin Watts is a division of Hachette Children's Books,
an Hachette UK company.
www.hachette.co.uk

Please note:
The names of the children featured in this book have been changed. The children's
answers to the young reporter's questions are personal and it should not be
assumed that all children in France have fun in exactly the same way.

CONTENTS

Sections marked with this symbol have free audio clips available at www.franklinwatts.co.uk/downloads

Ryan

MEET RYAN, OUR YOUNG REPORTER IN FRANCE

Meet Ryan. He is in France on a special mission. He is going to find out how children have fun in France. He has lots of questions.

What type of music do French children listen to?

What do they get up to with their friends?

What sort of films do they like best?

What do they like doing in their free time?

What is **la bande dessinée?**

What games do they play?

Read on and find out the answers to these questions... *and lots more!*

BIENVENUE EN FRANCE!

Welcome to France!
The little town of Crest is in south-east France.
Meet some children who live there.

CREST

Antoine is 11.

He lives with his mum and dad, his two sisters and his dog, Bonbon.

He loves all sports... or almost all.

What is his secret passion? You'll find out later!

Antoine

Romain is 12.

He lives with his parents and younger brother, Léo.

He loves music and playing computer games.

He speaks French and English. He's learning a third language. Which one?

Romain

Did you know?

French children between the ages of 8 and 12 spend 40% of their time in front of a screen!

Juliette is 12.

She lives with her dad and younger brother, Jérémie.

She loves having fun with her friends.

Find out what her secret ambition is!

Juliette

You can practise your French and learn some new words as you find out what these children have to say.

J'AIME LE SPORT

Today our young reporter is interviewing Antoine about the sports he likes.

Young reporter: **Salut, Antoine! Tu aimes quel sport?**

Antoine: **Mon sport préféré, c'est le canoë – et à l'école, c'est le handball.**

Canoeing (**le canoë-kayak**) is popular in France. The River Drôme, near Crest, is brilliant for canoeing. France has many rivers with plenty of opportunities for canoeing and white water rafting (**le rafting en eau vive**), sometimes in spectacular canyons.

J'aime bien le football. Je joue avec mes copains.

Je suis supporter de l'équipe de France. Allez la France!

USEFUL PHRASES

Tu aimes quel sport? What sport do you like?
Mon sport préféré, c'est... My favourite sport is... **à l'école** at school **C'est...** It is...
J'aime bien... I like... **Je joue** I play **avec mes copains** with my friends
Je suis supporter de l'équipe de... I support the... team **Allez!** Come on!

Antoine is really sporty! His favourite sport is canoeing, which he does at weekends. He likes swimming a lot too. At school, his favourite sport is handball. It is very popular in France where it is called **le handball** or **le hand** for short. It is a combination of basketball, football and netball, normally played on an indoor court by two teams of seven players. It is very fast: players can't hold the ball for more than three seconds without passing it. The object is to score goals into a net.

Like most of his friends, Antoine also loves football (**le football**). He and his dad support the French national team and watch all the matches on TV. His all-time favourite French footballers are Zinédine Zidane and Yoann Gourcuff.

Antoine plays tennis (**le tennis**) and badminton (**le badminton**) too, and he likes riding his bike (**le vélo**) and walking (**la marche**). He often takes his dog, Bonbon, for a walk. Are there any sports that Antoine doesn't like? He says, "**Je déteste le rugby!**" – he really hates rugby!

The top 10 favourite sports in France

football (**le football**)   tennis (**le tennis**)   judo (**le judo**)
French bowls (**la pétanque**)   basketball (**le basket**)   horseriding (**l'équitation**)
rugby (**le rugby**)   skiing (**le ski**)   golf (**le golf**)   sailing (**la voile**)

YOUR TURN   *Et toi, tu aimes quel sport?*

 J'aime le/la/l'....

 Je déteste le/la/l'....

Have you noticed that many names for sports are very similar in French and English?

SPORT IN FRANCE

If you love sport, then France is the place for you!

Sailing (la voile)

Sailing is popular and children learn in small boats called **des optimistes**. There are some famous races including **la Route du Rhum**, from France to the United States of America, and **le Tour de France à la voile**, from the English Channel to the Mediterranean Sea.

Breton 'boules' (la boule bretonne)

In order to win, a player must roll two large bowls nearest to the little ball, the jack (**le cochonnet**), which in French means piglet!

Cycling (le cyclisme)

Cycling is one of the most popular sports in France. The famous race **le Tour de France** takes place every year in July.

le Massif Central

les Alpes

Surfing (le surf)

The big waves on the French Atlantic coast make it one of the best places in the world for all sorts of surfing: **le surf, le bodyboard, le longboard, le kneeboard, le kite surf!**

les Pyrénées

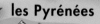

Pelota (la pelote basque)

Pelota is a game a bit like baseball, played only in this part of France. Players throw a ball against a wall with one hand and catch it with a sort of basket.

Rugby (le rugby)

Lots of rugby fans live in the south-west of France. The national team is called **les Bleus** (the Blues) or **les Tricolores** (the Three-colours): they wear blue, white and red kits (to match the colours of the French flag).

RUGBY FRANCE

Did you know?

The cockerel is the emblem of the French national football and rugby teams. Have you ever seen **Le Coq sportif** logo ('the sporty cockerel') on sports equipment and clothing?

Skiing *(le ski)*

The Alps and the Pyrenees have some of the best ski resorts in Europe, with more than 8,000 kilometres of ski slopes – that is eight times the length of France! They're also great for snowboarding **(le snowboard)** and tobogganing **(la luge)**.

A lot of sports were 'invented' in France: tennis, cycling, fencing, motor racing, even cricket! Recently, a young French firefighter developed a new sport, **le parkour**, where you climb and jump over obstacles, like walls and buildings.

Petanque *(la pétanque)*

This bowls game started out in Provence and originally meant 'both feet together'. Standing in a small circle, players throw metal bowls near the jack. Great fun for all the family!

MINI-QUIZ

Can you guess?

1 The order of difficulty of ski slopes?

 piste noire

piste verte

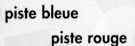 piste bleue

piste rouge

2 The colour of the jersey of the winner of **le Tour de France**?

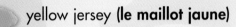 yellow jersey **(le maillot jaune)**

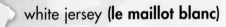 white jersey **(le maillot blanc)**

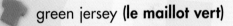 green jersey **(le maillot vert)**

3 Which sport each of these important events is famous for?

a. Roland-Garros tournament
b. les 24 heures du Mans
c. Prix de l'Arc de Triomphe

MINI-QUIZ ANSWERS

1 easy: green, medium: blue, difficult: red, very difficult: black
2 yellow jersey for winner – white is for the best newcomer, green for the best sprint points
3 a. tennis b. sports-car race c. horse racing

EXTRA CHALLENGE

Can you name a famous French sportsman or woman?

How many French footballers can you name?

VIVE LA MUSIQUE!

Today our young reporter is interviewing Romain about music and his rock band.

Young reporter: **Salut, Romain! Tu joues d'un instrument de musique?**

Romain: **Oui, je joue de la guitare électrique.**

Like most towns in France, Crest has a music school (**une école de musique**) where children can go and learn an instrument quite cheaply. Half of all French children play a musical instrument until they are 14. Serious young musicians can go to special schools called **conservatoires**, where they take music exams.

Je joue dans un groupe avec des copains. C'est génial!

USEFUL PHRASES

Tu joues d'un instrument de musique? Do you play a musical instrument?
Je joue... I play... **de la guitare électrique** the electric guitar **dans un groupe** in a band
avec des copains with some friends **C'est génial!** It's great!

Music is Romain's favourite pastime (**son passe-temps préféré**). He started classical guitar at music school on Wednesdays but quickly switched to electric guitar. It was his idea to start a rock band (**un groupe rock**) with the help of a music teacher (**un professeur de musique**). There are now six of them in the band called 'Crest-cendo', a play on words combining the name of their town, Crest, and the musical term, *crescendo*. They meet up at

Romain playing music with friends.

school for rehearsals (**les répétitions**) and sometimes play at school fêtes.

"**Je joue aussi du piano mais je suis nul!**" Romain says. He plays the piano, which his mum taught him, but he's no good at it. He still has a lot of fun playing it with his friends!

Crest is a great place for music. Every summer it has a music festival (**un festival**) called Crest Jazz Vocal, where famous jazz musicians perform. They also have concerts (**des concerts**) and workshops for 8-to-12-year olds. Romain can't wait for next summer's festival!

Popular instruments in France

electric guitar (**la guitare électrique**), classical guitar (**la guitare classique**), piano (**le piano**), flute (**la flûte**), violin (**le violon**), drums (**la batterie**), saxophone (**le saxophone**), trumpet (**la trompette**) harp (**la harpe**)

YOUR TURN

Et toi? Tu joues d'un instrument de musique?

✔ *Oui, je joue du/ de la...*

✘ *Non, je ne joue pas d'instrument.*

Some instruments start with **la**: **Je joue de la flûte.** Others start with **le**: **Je joue du piano.** Watch out! **de + le = du.**

13

THE MUSIC SCENE

What music do French children listen to?

French children like rap (**le rap**), hip hop (**le hip hop**), RnB (**le RnB**), rock (**le rock**) and techno (**la techno**). They are likely to know all the groups and singers you like too! Generally, French children are not very keen on classical music (**la musique classique**).

Most children love French pop music (**la variété française**). Outside France, songs in French are not as popular as those in English, so you might not have heard any of them. In France, World music from French-speaking countries in Africa, North Africa and the Caribbean is also very popular.

MC Solaar, one of the first French rappers

Faites la Fête!

On 21 June it is Music Day in France: **la Fête de la Musique**. Professional and amateur musicians perform in street shows (above), cafés and concert halls.

The French love music festivals: there are over 2,000 of them every year all over the country, including some just for kids, such as **les Francos Juniors** in July in la Rochelle, a city in western France, at the time of the world-famous **Francofolies** festival (left).

Cool classics

French composer Camille Saint-Saëns wrote *The Carnival of the Animals* (**le Carnaval des Animaux**), which uses music to represent different farm or wild animals. Some of his music was used in the famous film, *Babe*.

Paul Dukas composed *The Sorcerer's Apprentice* (**l'Apprenti sorcier**), made famous by Mickey Mouse in the Disney film, *Fantasia*.

Did you know?

Paris's Museum of Music (**la Cité de la Musique**) has the tallest string instrument ever made, **l'octobasse**, at 3.48 metres high!

Did you know?

In French, the musical notes are called:

'do, ré, mi, fa, sol, la, si' =

C, D, E, F, G, A, B

MINI-QUIZ

Do you know?

1 Which instrument is usually associated with French music?

- la harpe
- l'accordéon
- le piano

2 What is the French national anthem called?

- la Bastille
- la Marseillaise
- Frère Jacques

3 Which world-famous French singer was nicknamed 'the Sparrow' because she was so small?

- Carla Bruni
- Edith Piaf
- Céline Dion

EXTRA CHALLENGE

How many French or French-speaking singers and musicians can you name?

COPAINS–COPINES

Today, Juliette tells Ryan how much she enjoys being with her friends.

Young reporter: **Salut, Juliette!**
Qu'est-ce que tu aimes faire avec tes copains et tes copines?

Juliette: **J'aime bien faire la fête et j'adore jouer à des jeux de société.**

Le jeu de Jungle Speed, c'est drôle!

Traditionally, in France, children's birthday parties take place at home, with outdoor games like a treasure hunt (**une chasse au trésor**), or indoor activities like arts and craft and games. Children eat birthday cake (**un gâteau d'anniversaire**) and sweets (**des bonbons**). The birthday boy or girl blows out the candles and opens gifts before guests leave.

Les fêtes d'anniversaire, j'adore ça!

USEFUL PHRASES

Qu'est-ce que tu aimes faire? What do you like doing ?
avec tes copains et tes copines with your friends   **J'aime bien...** I like...   **J'adore...** I love...
faire le fête to party   **jouer à** to play   **des jeux de société** board games
les fêtes d'anniversaire birthday parties   **C'est drôle** It's good fun   **J'adore ça!** I love it!

Juliette thinks friends are very important. On Wednesday afternoons and at the weekend, she loves getting together with her best friend Maria. They chat about everything and nothing: school, boys, clothes and things like that. They are both mad about reading and share their comic-strip collections. They both enjoy listening to music too, and playing it. They both play in Romain's band and they practise together before the rehearsals.

Juliette loves parties and she always has good ideas for games and activities. She got Romain some bubbles and balloons for his 12th birthday.

She likes organising games and karaoke (**les karaokés**), dancing (**danser**), fancy dress (**les déguisements**) and generally having fun!

Juliette's friends are mainly girls, but she has friends that are boys too. She gets on well with them. There is just one thing she does not really like doing with them. She says: "**Je n'aime pas jouer à la Play. Ça m'énerve!**" She doesn't like playing on the Playstation. It just gets on her nerves!

What do most French children do with their friends?

watching TV (**regarder la télé**)   playing video games (**jouer à des jeux vidéo**)
playing board games (**jouer à des jeux de société**)   chatting (**discuter**)
shopping (**faire du shopping**)

YOUR TURN

Et toi, qu'est-ce que tu aimes faire avec tes copains et tes copines?

 J'aime bien …

 Je n'aime pas …

To say you like something:
 J'aime…
To say you don't like something, you add **n'… pas**:
 Je n'aime pas…

FRIENDS RULE!

What do French kids get up to when they get together?

Like you, French kids like getting together and having fun with their friends at home. They like sleepovers (**les soirées pyjama**), girls especially! They chat, watch films and eat party food!

Sleepovers are great fun!

Favourite outings are paintballing (**le paintball**), laser games (**les jeux laser**) and cinema (**le cinéma**). In France, cinema tickets are cheap for children under the age of 12 and many can afford to pay with their pocket money.

Their favourite films are cartoons (**les dessins animés**), fantasy (**les films fantastiques**) like the 'Harry Potter' and 'Twilight' series, comedies (**les comédies**) and action films (**les films d'action**).

French children love going shopping for bits and pieces. If they can, they like to buy designer accessories for school, such as bags and pencil cases (left). They can also show off their designer clothes at school as they don't have to wear a uniform. A favourite French designer name is Little Marcel (right).

Over half of French 8-to-12-year-olds get some pocket money (**l'argent de poche**), of between 10 and 20 euros a month. They buy game cards (such as Pokémon) and board games, clothes and accessories, sweets and snacks and presents for friends.

About a third of them manage to save some of their money! Do you?

Did you know?

The money used in France is the euro (before 2000, it was the franc).

Euro banknotes are the same for all European countries that use the euro.

Euro coins are only the same on one side. Euros made in France have one side that is typically French.

MINI-QUIZ

Do you know?

1 Which French inventors invented cinema?

- the Montgolfier brothers
- the Lumière brothers
- Pierre and Marie Curie

2 What symbol of France is on French euro coins?

- a lady, called Marianne
- a cockerel
- the Eiffel Tower

3 Which of these clothing labels is not French?

- Little Marcel
- Adidas
- Le Coq Sportif

MINI-QUIZ ANSWERS

3 Adidas

2 a lady, called Marianne

1 the Lumière brothers

EXTRA CHALLENGE

Have you ever seen a French film or cartoon? Look for one of these on DVD – *La Gloire de mon Père, Les Choristes, Kirikou,* or *L'illusionniste*. Most have subtitles.

DANS MA CHAMBRE

Today, Romain tells our young reporter what he has got in his bedroom.

Young reporter: **Alors, Romain, qu'est-ce que tu as dans ta chambre?**

Romain: **J'ai une Play. Je joue beaucoup à FIFA. C'est génial!**

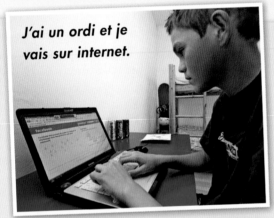

J'ai un ordi et je vais sur internet.

Video games, the internet and television are the top three pastimes for 8-to-12-year olds in France. Nine out of ten boys play video games (though only six out of ten girls) for about six hours a week.

Children spend about four hours a week on the internet. They keep in touch with their friends using their favourite social networks.

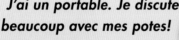

J'ai un portable. Je discute beaucoup avec mes potes!

USEFUL PHRASES

Qu'est-ce que tu as dans ta chambre? What have you got in your bedroom?
j'ai... I have... **une Play** a Playstation **un ordi** a computer **un portable** a mobile
je joue beaucoup I play a lot **je vais sur internet** I go on the internet
je discute beaucoup I chat a lot **avec mes potes** with my mates

20

Romain is never bored at home. In his bedroom, he plays video games and uses the internet a lot to contact his friends by email (**par mail**) or on social networks. Like many French children, he has a blog (**un blog**) where he shares music and photos of his band. He also sends his friends loads of text messages (**des SMS**)!

Romain says, "**J'écoute beaucoup de musique.**" He listens to music a lot: he downloads his favourite tracks onto his laptop and

Like Hugo, Romain would be lost without his laptop!

shares them with his friend Hugo. He also watches clips of his favourite bands on youtube or dailymotion.fr. His favourite radio station is **Skyrock**, because he loves the music they play. The other radio station French children like is **NRJ** (this sounds like 'energy' when you say the letters in French!).

Romain adds: "**Je ne regarde pas beaucoup la télé.**" He doesn't watch a lot of TV. He prefers watching DVDs (**des DVD**) on his laptop and he quite likes reading (**la lecture**). He often swaps magazines, comics and books with Juliette.

In French children's bedrooms:

a computer (**un ordinateur** or **ordi**)   a television (**une télévision** or **télé**)
a games console (**une console de jeux**)   a CD player (**un lecteur de CD**)
a radio (**une radio**)   an MP3 player (**un baladeur**)   an iPod (**un iPod**)
a docking station (**un dock radio-réveil**)   a Wii (**une Wii**)

YOUR TURN

Et toi, qu'est-ce que tu as dans ta chambre?

 Dans ma chambre, j'ai ...

French text language (**le langage SMS**)
bjr = **bonjour** (hello)
slt = **salut** (hi)
stp = **s'il te plaît** (pls)
mrc = **merci** (thx)
mdr = **mort de rire** (lol)
a2m1 = **à demain** (c u 2mro)
a+ = **à plus** (c u l8r)
biz = **bises** (kiss xx)

QUIET TIME!

What do French children do in their free time at home?

French children like watching the same TV programmes as you... but dubbed in French! They love game shows, American series and reality TV shows like **Star Academy**, the French version of *Pop Idol*. A lot of them follow the first successful French soap **Plus Belle La Vie**.

However, the favourite pastime for French 8-to-12-year-olds is reading. There are over 70 magazines (**les magazines**) for children and teens, even a few for babies! Among the most popular are **Astrapi** and **Okapi** (news and general interest), **Science et Vie Junior** and **Géo Ado** (*Science and the World*). Girls like **Les P'tites Sorcières**, **Julie** (general interest, news and quizzes) and **Cheval Star** (about horses), while boys prefer sports magazines like **France Football** or **Onze**.

Comic strips (**les bandes dessinées** or **les BD**) are extremely popular in France, with both children and adults. The best-known comic strips in French are *Astérix*, *Tintin*, *les Schtroumpfs*, *Lucky Luke*, *Titeuf* and *Gaston Lagaffe*. French children also love *The Simpsons* and Japanese mangas (**les manga**), like *Naruto*.

Did you know?

Comic strips have their own museum and international festival in Angoulême, in the centre of France.

Among the most famous classic French books for children are **Le Petit Prince**, by Antoine de Saint-Exupéry, and **Le Petit Nicolas**, by Goscinny.

Max et Lili, a series about the life of two ten-year-olds, has over 90 titles which French children love collecting!

Anya fait une collection de peluches.

Children like collecting things (**faire une collection**). They collect games cards (**des cartes**) like Yu-Gi-Oh!, Pokémon, Naruto, Dragon Ball or Titeuf, soft toys (**des peluches**), manga or Warhammer figures (**des figurines**), miniature cars (**des petites voitures**), stamps (**des timbres**) and key rings (**des porte-clés**).

MINI-QUIZ

Can you guess?

1 Where you can borrow books in France?

- la librairie
- la bibliothèque
- la maison de la presse

2 The name of Asterix's best friend?

- Milou
- Idéfix
- Obélix

3 What **un stickophile** collects?

- lipstick
- stickers
- bookmarks

MINI-QUIZ ANSWERS

3 stickers

2 Obélix

1 la bibliothèque

EXTRA CHALLENGE

Have you ever watched something in French?

Try some short videos and clips online at

http://videos.tf1.fr/programmes-tv-jeunesse/

MA PASSION SECRÈTE

Today, young reporter Ryan is asking some of the children from Crest if they have any special interests, unusual hobbies or secret passions!

Young reporter: **Est-ce que tu as une passion secrète?**

Romain: **Le mercredi, j'apprends le chinois. Mon rêve, c'est visiter la Chine.**

Juliette: **Le mercredi, j'apprends le dessin. Mon rêve, c'est dessiner des BD!**

In France, Wednesday (**le mercredi**) is a special day for children: most primary school children have the whole day off and in secondary school, they don't have lessons in the afternoon. It's the day for chores (like visits to the doctor or the dentist) and some children might go to religious education classes. However, most have a busy schedule of leisure activities and time to enjoy their favourite hobby!

Antoine: **Moi, j'apprends le jardinage avec mon grand-père. J'aime trop la nature!**

USEFUL PHRASES

Est-ce que tu as... Do you have... **une passion secrète** a secret passion
j'apprends... I'm learning... **le chinois** Chinese **le dessin** drawing
le jardinage gardening **Mon rêve, c'est...** My dream is... **visiter la Chine** to visit China
dessiner des BD to draw comic strips **j'aime trop...** I just love...

On Wednesday afternoons, Romain has Chinese lessons (**des leçons de chinois**). He is fascinated by China and is really enthusiastic about learning the language. It is hard work but he loves it! He also has time to do some DIY (**le bricolage**) with his dad, which he loves.

Juliette loves cooking. That's lucky as she often has to cook on Wednesdays when her dad is away for work. He gave her a great recipe book (**un livre de recettes**) for Christmas. Today, Juliette made some **quenelles**, a local speciality made with meat and semolina.

Mon rêve, c'est travailler avec des animaux.

Antoine loves nature and animals. As Bonbon, his dog, is a bit unruly, he takes him to dog training near Crest on Wednesdays. His dream is to work with animals when he grows up.

Some interesting pastimes:

cooking (**la cuisine**) DIY (**le bricolage**) gardening (**le jardinage**)
sewing (**la couture**) learning languages (**les langues**)
fishing (**la pêche**) kite flying (**le cerf-volant**)

YOUR TURN

Et toi? Est-ce que tu as une passion secrète?

J'aime trop le/la/les …

Listen to the audio file: Est-ce que (often used to ask yes/no questions) sounds like 'eska'.

SERIOUS FUN!

From juggling to politics, there is a wide choice of leisure activities in France.

On Wednesdays, a lot of French children go to a day centre (**un centre de loisirs**) to do arts and crafts, sports, drama and sometimes more unusual – and very French – activities such as puppetry (**les marionnettes**), miming (**le mime**) and circus skills such as juggling (**le jonglage**) or clowning!

Some children enjoy more 'serious' pastimes. In many French towns, children can elect their representatives on a children's local council (**le conseil municipal d'enfants**). For two years, they meet twice a month and attend one or two council meetings with the mayor at the Town Hall. They really do get to influence local life, for instance by improving play areas in parks. Some are even sent to the French Parliament (**l'Assemblée Nationale**) in Paris.

LIBERTE EGALITE FRATERNITE

HOTEL DE VILLE

Le jonglage, c'est super!

Did you know?

RF on official buildings stands for **République Française** (French Republic).

More and more schoolchildren, like Romain's friend Camille, are enjoying joint activities with old people (**les personnes âgées**). Camille says that there is so much you can learn about how things used to be and so much you can teach them, such as how to cope with modern technology!

 During **la Semaine Bleue** (the blue week), young and old do things together.

Culture is a very important aspect of French life and children are encouraged to visit museums (**les musées**). All national museums are free for under 18s and provide special activities for children on Wednesdays and at weekends.

MINI-QUIZ

1 Which of these French museums is the most visited?

- le Château de Versailles
- le Musée du Louvre
- le Musée Picasso

2 Match the name to the description.

a) traditional French puppet

b) a world famous French mime artist

c) a traditional clown with a white face

 Pierrot

 Guignol

 Marcel Marceau

3 Did you spot the French word for Town Hall on page 26?

MINI-QUIZ ANSWERS

3 l'hôtel de ville

2 a Guignol,
b Marcel Marceau, **c** Pierrot

1 Le Musée du Louvre

EXTRA CHALLENGE

Do you know who is the President of the French Republic?

TEST YOUR MEMORY!

1 Which sport is very popular in French schools?

- bowls
- handball
- parkour

2 What is the symbol of the French rugby and football teams?

- a frog
- a cockerel
- an eagle

3 When is music celebrated all over France?

- on 21 June
- on 14 July
- once a month

4 Which of these is a famous French comic book?

- Astrapi
- Astérix
- Skyrock

5 How much pocket money do most French children have?

- less than 10 euros a month
- between 10 and 20 euros
- more than 20 euros

6 What do French children call a Playstation?

- un ordi
- une Play
- un jeu

7 What are Skyrock and NRJ?

- French TV channels
- French radio stations
- French magazines

8 What does this text mean? 'Slt! A2m1. Biz'

- Hi! You ok? Bye
- Hi! C u l8r, X
- Hi! C u 2mro, X

INTERESTING WEBSITES

- **Watch a video about an annual sporting event:** http://www.bbc. co.uk/learningzone/clips/jours-de-sport-marseille/5701.html

- **Find out about musical instruments in French:** http://artsalive.ca/fr/mus/instrumentlab/

- **Listen to children sing in French and follow the words:** http://www.csdraveurs. qc.ca/musique/choralies/karaokes.htm

- **Play games to practise counting euros:** http://www.momes.net/education/mesure/exercices/euro.html

- **Find out more about French children's magazines. Click on covers and turn the pages!** http://www.bayard-jeunesse.com/presse-magazines/feuilletez.jsp?lblorig=BJ_ST_JEUN_Standard

- **Explore the website of a French TV channel for children (play games, watch videos, etc):** http://www.m6kid.fr/home.php

- **Watch what happens when young delegates go to the French parliament:** http://www.parlementdesenfants.fr/le-parlement-des-enfants-c-est-quoi

Note to parents and teachers: Every effort has been made by the Publishers to ensure that these websites are suitable for children, that they are of the highest educational value, and that they contain no inappropriate or offensive material. However, because of the nature of the Internet, it is impossible to guarantee that the contents of these sites will not be altered. We strongly advise that Internet access is supervised by a responsible adult.

TRANSLATIONS

Pages 8–9

J'aime le sport.

I like sport.

Salut, Antoine! Tu aimes quel sport?

Hi Antoine! Which sports do you like?

Mon sport préféré, c'est le canoë – et à l'école, c'est le handball.

My favourite sport is canoeing and at school, it's handball.

J'aime bien le football. Je joue avec mes copains.

I like football. I play with my friends.

Je suis supporter de l'équipe de France. Allez la France!

I support the French team. Come on, France!

Je déteste le rugby! I hate rugby!

Et toi, tu aimes quel sport?

What about you? Which sport do you like?

J'aime le/la/l'… I like…

Je déteste le/la/l'… I hate …

Pages 12–13

Vive la musique! Music's great!

Salut, Romain! Tu joues d'un instrument de musique?

Hi Romain! Do you play a musical instrument?

Oui, je joue de la guitare électrique.

Yes, I play the electric guitar.

Je joue dans un groupe avec des copains. C'est génial!

I play in a band with some friends. It's great!

Je joue aussi du piano mais je suis nul!

I also play the piano but I'm no good at it!

Et toi? Tu joues d'un instrument de musique?

What about you? Do you play a musical instrument?

Oui, je joue du/ de la... Yes, I play the...

Non, je ne joue pas d'instrument.

No, I don't play an instrument.

Pages 16–17

Copains-Copines Friends

Salut, Juliette! Qu'est-ce que tu aimes faire avec tes copains et tes copines?

Hi, Juliette! What do you like doing with your friends?

J'aime bien faire la fête et j'adore jouer à des jeux de société.

I like parties and I love playing board games.

Le jeu de Jungle Speed, c'est drôle!

The Jungle Speed game is good fun.

Les fêtes d'anniversaire, j'adore ça!

I just love birthday parties!

Et toi, qu'est-ce que tu aimes faire avec tes copains et tes copines?

What about you? What do you like doing with your friends?

J'aime bien…
I like…

Je n'aime pas…
I don't like…

Pages 20–21

Dans ma chambre
In my bedroom.

Alors, Romain, qu'est-ce que tu as dans ta chambre?
So Romain, what have you got in your bedroom?

J'ai une Play. Je joue beaucoup à FIFA. C'est génial!
I have a PlayStation. I play FIFA a lot. It's great!

J'ai un ordi et je vais sur internet.
I have a laptop and I go on the internet.

J'ai un portable. Je discute beaucoup avec mes potes!
I have a mobile phone. I chat with my mates a lot!

J'écoute beaucoup de musique.
I listen to a lot of music.

Je ne regarde pas beaucoup la télé.
I don't watch a lot of TV.

Et toi, qu'est-ce que tu as dans ta chambre?
What about you? What have you got in your bedroom?

Dans ma chambre, j'ai…
In my bedroom, I have…

Pages 24–25

Ma passion secrète My secret passion

Est-ce que tu as une passion secrète?
Do you have a secret passion?

Le mercredi, j'apprends le chinois. Mon rêve, c'est visiter la Chine.
On Wednesdays, I'm learning Chinese. My dream is to visit China.

Le mercredi, j'apprends le dessin. Mon rêve, c'est dessiner des BD!
On Wednesdays, I'm learning how to draw My dream is to draw comic strips!

Moi, j'apprends le jardinage avec mon grand-père. J'aime trop la nature!
I'm learning gardening with my grandfather. I just love nature!

Mon rêve, c'est travailler avec des animaux.
My dream is to work with animals.

Et toi? Est-ce que tu as une passion secrète?
What about you? Do you have a secret passion?

J'aime trop le/la/les …
I just love…

INDEX

TEST YOUR FRENCH

Can you remember what these words mean?

1 Mes copains: my books? my friends? my games?

2 Les dessins animés: cartoons? comic strips? drawing?

3 L'argent de poche: board game? pocket money? pastime?

4 Un portable: laptop? mobile? video game?

5 La lecture: playing? collecting? reading?

1. Mes copains: my friends 2. Les dessins animés: cartoons 3. l'argent de poche: pocket money 4. Un portable: mobile 5. La lecture: reading